LOOK 4

A reading anthology for young learners

KAJ SCHWERMER

NATIONAL GEOGRAPHIC

L E A R N I N G

Australia • Brazil • Mexico • Singapore • United Kingdom • United States

Contents

Firefighters of Edo

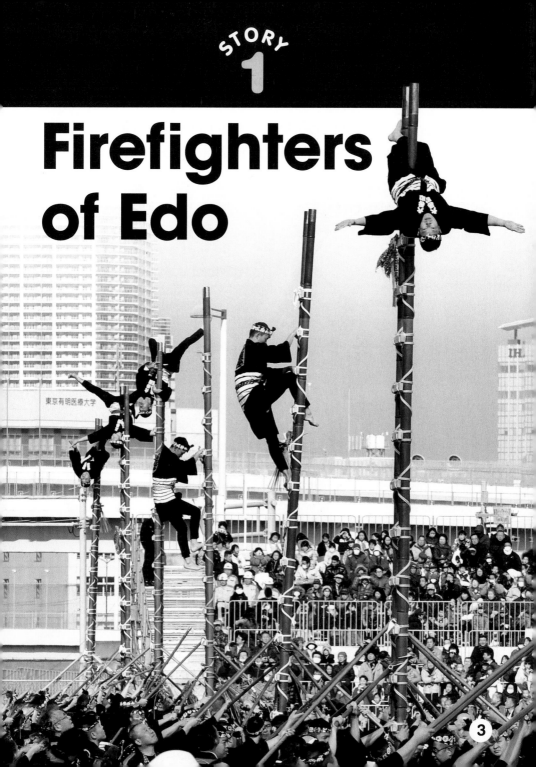

These days, firefighters around the world use very modern equipment, including robots, oxygen tanks, huge fire engines, helmets and hoses made of the latest material. Three hundred years ago, in the city of Edo in Japan, things were very different. Today this city is called Tokyo.

Edo was once a small, Japanese fishing village but it got bigger and bigger. Three hundred years ago, Edo was the biggest city in the world. More than one million people lived there. There weren't any cars, so the streets of Edo were very narrow and the houses were very close together. Nearly all the houses were made of wood and bamboo with paper doors and straw roofs.

Summers were very hot and winters were very dry in Edo. People used fire to cook and oil lamps to light their houses at night. There were lots of fires in Edo. There were also lots of firefighters. They were called *hikeshi* in Japanese. There weren't any robots, oxygen tanks, fire engines, helmets or hoses. In fact, there wasn't even much water! So, how did the *hikeshi* in Edo do their job?

Firefighters in Edo used special tools, like hooks and bamboo ladders, to fight fires and pull down buildings.

The *hikeshi* had special jackets, or *hanten*. They were very thick and heavy. Each fire station had its own special jacket. It had the fire station's symbol on the back and on the inside there was a colourful painting. You can see this jacket in the Tokyo Fire Museum.

Each fire station had its own special banner, or *matoi*, with the fire station's symbol at the top.

When there was a fire, firefighters from the nearest fire station raced to the building on fire. One brave firefighter climbed onto the roof, holding the *matoi*, so that the other firefighters could see exactly where the fire was.

The *matoi* was so important that the firefighter on the roof didn't let it go. The other firefighters tried to put out the fire very quickly so that he didn't get hurt.

These days, firefighters spray water on fires from hoses or from huge fire engines.

In Edo, however, it was difficult for the firefighters to find enough water, so they used a very different technique to fight big fires. Instead of trying to put out the fire in a burning building, they destroyed the buildings next to it to stop the fire spreading.

People gathered around to watch the firefighters of Edo in action. It was very entertaining to watch them do acrobatics on the ladders. It was so popular that even today in Japan we can see acrobats performing at festivals every year.

Diego and the table

A long time ago, in Costa Rica, there was a woman who lived with her two sons. The youngest son, Diego, was an honest boy, but he didn't understand the value of money.

They were very poor. One year, they had a very bad year. Their corn dried up, so they couldn't make any tortillas. Their beans didn't grow, so they couldn't eat beans with their rice.

One day, the woman called her sons and said, 'Boys, take our cow to the market and sell it. Make sure you get lots of money for it.'

'OK,' said Diego. 'Don't worry, Mother.'

The two sons walked through the forest to the market with the cow. When they arrived, the older brother went to buy some things.

'Stay here with our cow,' he said to Diego.

While the older brother was away, a young man
passed Diego with a big table.

'Hello,' he said. 'Why are you here with your cow?'

'I'm going to sell it at the market,' replied Diego.

'Don't sell it,' said the young man. 'Why don't you
swap it for my table?'

'OK!' said Diego. 'You take the cow and let me
have the table.'

After a while, Diego's brother returned.

'Where's the cow? Did you sell it?' he asked.

'No, I didn't. I swapped it for this table!' replied Diego proudly.

The brother was angry. 'For a table? What are we going to tell Mother?'

The two boys started to walk home. Diego could only walk very slowly with the table on his back. It started to get dark, so they decided to sleep in a big tree where it was safe. They didn't want to leave the table on the ground, so Diego carried the table up into the tree.

Suddenly, they could hear loud voices below.

Four men stopped under the tree, opened a big bag of silver coins and started to count them.

'Shh!' the older brother whispered. 'They're robbers! Those coins are from the market! Oh no! I hope they don't see us.'

Diego still had the table on his back. He started to get tired and said quietly, 'This table is very heavy.'

'Be quiet!' whispered his brother. 'Don't drop it!'

But Diego couldn't hold the table any longer. He closed his eyes and dropped it. With a terrible noise, it landed right in the middle of the robbers. They believed it was a wild animal and hurried away, leaving the silver coins behind.

The two brothers climbed down and picked up all the coins. They carried the coins back to the market and gave them back to the merchants.

The merchants were so grateful that they gave the brothers half of the coins. They carried the coins and the table home to their mother. Now they were rich and the family lived happily for many years.

A weekend in Dubai

It's Thursday afternoon and Manal and her twin sister, Huda, are very excited. You see, in Dubai, the school week ends on Thursday. Students have Friday and Saturday off.

Their teacher, Ms Haddad, tells the students, 'For homework, please write a journal about your weekend. Let's see who has the most exciting weekend!'

At home, the twins make lists of all the exciting things they want to do. They show their lists to their mum.

'This weekend, can we ... Oh! What are you doing?' they ask.

'I'm preparing some ingredients,' their mum answers. 'This weekend we're going to stay at home. We're going to make *luqaimat*, read books and study.'

'Oh, Mum! But we need to have an adventure this weekend to write about for homework!'

'Well, OK, let me talk to Dad later,' says Mum.

The next morning at breakfast, Mum and Dad say,
'We've got a surprise for you! Let's go out today and
have an adventure!'

'Oh, great! Thank you!' say the girls. 'What shall we do?'

'How about a ride on a speedboat?' says Dad.

'Wow! I love boats!' says Huda.

'Me too!' says Dad.

They go to the marina and get in a speedboat. Dad drives the boat. The boat is very fast. Everyone is very happy.

'Look! There's the Palm Jumeirah!' shouts Huda.

'Can you see the World Islands? They're some of the most amazing islands in Dubai!' says Manal.

They go past the Burj Al Arab Hotel on the way back to the marina.

'That's one of the most beautiful hotels in Dubai,' says Mum.

'That was fun!' says Huda. 'Where can we go next?'

'How about a drive in the desert?' says Dad.

They drive out to the desert and ride quad bikes over the sand dunes.

'That was great,' says Manal, 'but I'm hot now.'

'I've got an idea!' says Huda. 'Let's go skiing!'

They drive to the Mall of the Emirates and go to the big indoor ski slope there.

'Wow!' says Dad. 'This is great! Look at me! Wheee!' He skis past Mum and the children very quickly.

'Look at the penguins! I love penguins! I think they're the funniest birds,' says Manal.

'That was so much fun!' says Dad. 'Who wants to go up the Burj Khalifa now?'

'Oh, yes, please!' say the children.

'Did you know it's the tallest building in the world?' says Mum.

'Wow! I'm sure there's an amazing view from up there!' says Manal.

They get into their car. Dad is still very excited.

'Where do you want to go next? I'm having so much fun!' asks Dad.

'Dad,' Mum and the girls all say together. 'We're tired! Can we go home now?'

Later, at home, they all make *luqaimat* together.
A delicious smell fills the air. Then they sit in the
living room, read books and study.

'This was the best day ever,' Manal and Huda
tell their mum and dad. 'We can't wait to write
about it in our journals tomorrow!'

The museum quiz

Marc and his sister, Carola, are watching TV. It's their favourite programme, *Top Quiz*. They watch *Top Quiz* every week. Now they're watching the news. There's a story about a big flood in Egypt. Lots of roads need rebuilding.

'We have to help them,' says Marc.

'I've got an idea!' says Carola. 'You're the best student in your class. Why don't you go on *Top Quiz*? If you win, you can send the prize money to Egypt.'

So Marc joins the show. Two months later, he's in the final!

'Hello. Welcome to this year's *Top Quiz* final. It's a special museum show, all about Berlin's famous Museum Island. I'm your host, Steve Swimmer. And here are the three finalists, Marc, Sophie and James.

Are you ready? Let's play *Top Quiz*!'

Marc is very nervous. The host asks the first question.

'Look at this picture. It's the famous Museum Island in Berlin. How many museums are there on the island?'

Marc answers first. 'That's easy. There are five museums on the island.'

'Correct!' says Steve.

'Ok, listen to the next question. In one museum you can see The Gate of Ishtar. It's from the city of Babylon and it's made of lapis lazuli bricks. What colour is this gate?'

This question is more difficult. Marc doesn't know the answer. Suddenly, the other boy answers.

'Lapis lazuli is blue, so I think the Gate of Ishtar is blue.'

'Correct! And here it is. Isn't it beautiful!' says Steve.

'Wow! Look at the animals on it!' says Marc.

'Right. Here's another question,' says Steve. 'This famous monument in the museum is from ancient Greece. Think about it. Can you remember its name?'

'Oh, I think I know that,' says Marc.

But, suddenly, the girl answers. 'I know! It's called the Pergamon Altar!'

'That's the correct answer!' says Steve.

'So everyone has got one point each. OK, listen carefully to the final question. The person who answers correctly is the winner!

In the New Museum on the island, there's a famous statue of Queen Nefertiti. Where was Queen Nefertiti from?'

No-one knows the answer.

'I have to have an answer, please,' says Steve. 'Does anyone know?'

Then, suddenly, Marc remembers why he wanted to be on *Top Quiz*.

'I know! She's from Egypt,' he cries.

'That's right, Marc. Congratulations! You're the new champion of the *Top Quiz* special museum show!' says Steve.

'Thank you! I'm so happy. I want to give the prize money to help the flood problem in Egypt.'

'That's great, Marc. Well done everyone!'

STORY 5

Superhero powers

Do you ever dream of having superpowers, like flying through outer space, being invisible, seeing around corners or climbing walls like a spider? Well, you're not the only one. Let's have a look at some of the people who are inventing technology that maybe one day will make these superpowers a reality.

Flying through outer space was something that only astronauts or comic book superheroes could do. Now, inventors and engineers are building rockets that someday anyone will be able to use.

This is SpaceX's most powerful rocket called The Falcon Heavy. But there are plans to build an even bigger rocket. The rocket will be bigger than a 12-storey building and more powerful than 100 jumbo jets!

Most of us know about rockets, but did you know that there are other people inventing technologies that give us superpowers as well?

Many superheroes use the power of invisibility. Scientists at Berkeley University in the US are developing an 'invisibility cloak'. The cloak is extremely thin. It's even thinner than a human hair! When it covers an object, it seems to make it disappear.

Berkeley University

So how does the cloak work?

There are many tiny, gold rectangles covering the thin material. They're all different sizes. The scientists covered a tiny object with the cloak and shone a special light on it. The gold rectangles on the cloak make it seem like the light is hitting a flat mirror. So the light is reflected back and the cloak and object look like they aren't even there.

For now, the cloak only works for tiny objects, but maybe one day in the future, it will work on bigger ones.

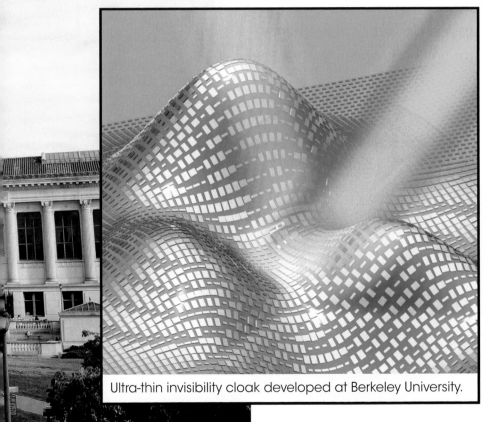

Ultra-thin invisibility cloak developed at Berkeley University.

Another superpower that people dream about is the ability to climb walls, like a spider.

Scientists at Stanford University and Draper Laboratory in the US are developing technology that allows anyone to climb a smooth wall using climbing paddles. The scientists looked at how a gecko climbs to inspire them. Geckos can climb walls and even hang upside down because they've got tiny hairs covering their feet.

Geckos can climb walls.

A gecko's foot has got tiny hairs on it.

The climbing paddles consist of two plates that a climber holds. There are twenty-four small tiles on each plate. Each tile is about the same size as a postage stamp and has got tiny 'hairs' made of silicon rubber on it, just like a gecko's feet.

Engineers tested the technology by using it to climb a glass wall. It was like hooking the device into glass which is, of course, impossible because glass is perfectly smooth.

A climber testing the Draper climbing paddles.

Just imagine if we could see around corners, like a superhero. Researchers at Massachusetts Institute of Technology (or MIT) in the US are working on technology that uses a smartphone camera to detect moving objects around corners. The system is called CornerCamera. One day we will probably use this system in cars, lorries and buses to save lives by detecting moving objects or people that a driver can't see.

So thanks to all this amazing, new technology, maybe our dreams of having superpowers will one day come true!

Maybe one day we'll be able to see around corners, like this one.

The king and the drums

A long time ago in India, there was a king who lived
high on a hill above the tamarind forest. The king
was very vain. He always dressed in the finest clothes.
There was a mirror in every room in the palace so he
could admire himself all day long.

The king was so vain he didn't care about the
people in his kingdom or their problems. He only
cared about his hair and his clothes.

The king changed his hairstyle every day. He always made sure it covered his ears. You see, the king had a terrible secret. His ears looked like donkey ears! The king didn't want to show his donkey ears to anyone. He only showed his ears to his barber, Baiju.

'You must promise to keep this a secret,' said the king.

'I promise,' replied Baiju.

Baiju didn't want to tell anyone the king's secret, so he moved away from the city to a house in the forest. He stopped cutting other people's hair. He stopped visiting his friends. He only talked to his wife, Gori.

Baiju wasn't happy. One day, Baiju and Gori were in the forest. The tamarind trees were all around.

Gori asked her husband, 'You're the king's barber and you're famous across the land, but you seem so unhappy. Tell me, dear, what's the matter?'

'I should keep it a secret, but there isn't anyone here except you and the tamarind trees, so I will tell you,' Baiju replied.

Then Baiju whispered his secret to her. Only the trees could hear his words.

'I won't tell anyone,' promised Gori.

Later that year, the king's musicians visited the forest. They used some branches from the tamarind trees to make their drums for the royal festival.

On the day of the festival, the musicians started to play their drums. Everyone was very surprised. Instead of music, they could hear the drums say, 'The king has got donkey ears!'

The king was very angry and said to Baiju, 'You haven't kept your promise! You've told everyone about my ears!'

Baiju was shocked and replied, 'I haven't told anyone except my wife. Only she and the tamarind trees have heard my words!'

The king asked the people in his kingdom if this was true. Everyone said it was true.

Suddenly, the wise queen said, 'You shouldn't hide your ears. Everyone will love you even with donkey ears. But you should be a good king and take care of your people.'

The king listened carefully and, with tears in his eyes, said, 'Yes, that's true. I'm sorry for only caring about how I look. I'll keep these drums in my room. They will remind me that I should always be a good king.'

Activities

STORY 1 Firefighters of Edo

1 Read and write T (Today) or E (Edo).

1 Firefighters spray water on fires from hoses or from huge fire engines. __T__

2 Firefighters used hooks and bamboo ladders to fight fires and pull down buildings. _____

3 Firefighters destroyed the buildings next to a burning building. _____

4 Each fire station had its own special jacket. _____

5 Firefighters use robots, oxygen tanks, huge fire engines, helmets and hoses. _____

2 Find the words in bold in the story. Circle the meaning.

1 A **narrow** street is (very small) / very big from one side to the other.

2 When the firefighters **raced** to the fire, they went very slowly / very quickly.

3 When firefighters **put out** a fire, they make the fire stop / get bigger.

4 The **roof** of a building is on top / on the side of the building.

5 A **brave** firefighter will run away from / go towards danger.

STORY 2 Diego and the table

1 Order the sentences from 1 to 7.

A They decided to sleep in a big tree. ☐

B One year the family had a very bad year. 1

C They carried the coins back to the market. ☐

D The two sons walked through the forest to the market with the cow. ☐

E Diego closed his eyes and dropped the table. ☐

F Diego swapped the cow for a table. ☐

G Four men stopped under the tree. ☐

2 Read and answer.

1 What kind of boy was Diego? _____

2 Why did the boys take the cow to the market?

_____

3 Why was Diego's brother angry?

_____

4 Why did Diego carry the table up into the tree?

_____

5 What did the boys do with the coins?

_____

A weekend in Dubai

1 Read and match.

1 They look at some penguins.	In the desert
2 They learn about their homework.	From a speedboat
3 They see an amazing view.	At school
4 They make *luqaimat*, read books and study.	In the indoor ski slope
5 They see some beautiful islands.	From the tallest building
6 They ride quad bikes.	At home

2 Read and answer.

1 What day of the week does school end in Dubai?

_____

2 What do the twins want to do this weekend?

_____

3 What does Mum say about the Burj Al Arab Hotel?

_____

4 What kind of bird does Manal love?

_____

5 What does Mum say about the Burj Khalifa?

_____

The museum quiz

1 Read and write the number.

1 The Pergamon Altar
2 The statue of Queen Nefertiti
3 The Berlin Museum Island
4 The Gate of Ishtar

A

B

C  1

D

2 Read and circle *True* or *False*.

1	There was a big flood in Egypt.	(True)	False
2	The Museum Island in Berlin has got four museums.	True	False
3	The Pergamon Altar is from ancient Greece.	True	False
4	The Gate of Ishtar is blue.	True	False
5	Queen Nefertiti was from Greece.	True	False

Superhero powers

1 Match the people and the technology.

1 Engineers at SpaceX
2 Scientists at Berkeley University
3 Scientists at Stanford University
4 Researchers at MIT

A invisibility cloak

B CornerCamera

C rockets

D climbing paddles

2 Read and answer.

1 What is SpaceX's most powerful rocket at the moment called?

_____

2 What is the invisibility cloak thinner than?

_____

3 What animal inspired the scientists to develop the climbing paddles?

_____

4 What have the climbing paddles got on them?

_____

5 What does the CornerCamera system use to detect moving objects around corners?

_____

STORY 6 The king and the drums

1 Read and circle.

1 The king's secret was that he:

   A was too handsome.
   B couldn't play the drums.
   C had donkey ears.

2 The drums were made of:

   A plastic.   **B** tamarind wood.   **C** metal.

3 Baiju was unhappy because he:

   A had donkey ears too.
   B couldn't tell anyone the king's secret.
   C was too famous.

4 In the end, the king:

   A realised he should be a better king.
   B moved to another castle.
   C looked in the mirror.

2 Read and answer.

1 What could the tamarind trees hear?

_____

2 Why was the king angry with Baiju?

_____

3 What did the queen tell the king to do at the end?

_____

National Geographic Learning,
a Cengage Company

Look 4: A reading anthology for young learners
Kaj Schwermer

Publisher: Sherrise Roehr

Publishing Consultant: Karen Spiller

Director of Global Marketing: Ian Martin

Heads of Regional Marketing:
Charlotte Ellis (Europe, Middle East and Africa)
Kiel Hamm (Asia)
Irina Pereyra (Latin America)

Product Marketing Manager: David Spain

Senior Director of Production: Michael Burggren

Senior Content Project Manager: Nick Ventullo

Media Researchers: Leila Hishmeh, Jeff Millies

Art Director: Brenda Carmichael

Manufacturing Buyer: Elaine Bevan

Composition: SPi Global

For permission to use material from this text or product,
submit all requests online at **cengage.com/permissions**
Further permissions questions can be emailed to
permissionrequest@cengage.com

ISBN: 978-0-357-02157-6

National Geographic Learning
Cheriton House, North Way,
Andover, Hampshire, SP10 5BE
United Kingdom

Locate your local office at **international.cengage.com/region**

Visit National Geographic Learning online at **ELTNGL.com**
Visit our corporate website at **www.cengage.com**

Credits

Cover: © O Chul Kwon.

Photos: 3 © KAZUHIRO NOGI/AFP/Getty Images; **4** © Monty Rakusen/Cultura/Getty Images; **5** © A. Burkatovski/Fine Art Images/SuperStock; **7** World Discovery/Alamy Stock Photo; **9** © Stockbyte/Getty Images; **10** © Saethapoeng TRIECHORB/Shutterstock.com; **11** © CHAPUT Franck/hemispicture.com/Getty Images; **21** © Ashraf Jandali/Shutterstock.com; **31** © Graham Lucas Commons/Photolibrary/Getty Images; **34** Bildagentur-online/Klein/Alamy Stock Photo; **36** Peter Horree/Alamy Stock Photo; **37** Hemis/Alamy Stock Photo; **38** © Vladimir Wrangel/Shutterstock.com; **41** © Draper Laboratories; **42–43** © SpaceX; **44–45** © Yurim/Shutterstock.com; **45** Xinhua/Alamy Stock Photo; **46** (l) © Mr.B-king/Shutterstock.com; **46** (r) © MonthiraYodtiwong/iStock/Getty Images; **47** (l) © Kusska/Shutterstock.com; **47** (r) © Draper Laboratories; **48** © kirill_makarov/Shutterstock.com; **49** © Jody Macdonald/National Geographic Creative; **61** (tl) Bildagentur-online/Klein/Alamy Stock Photo; **61** (tr) Peter Horree/Alamy Stock Photo; **61** (bl) Hemis/Alamy Stock Photo; **61** (br) © Vladimir Wrangel/Shutterstock.com.

Illustrations: 6–8 J.T. Morrow/Illustration Online; **11–20** Martin Bustamante/Advocate Art; **21–30** Aleksander Zolotic/Bright Group; **31–40** Andy Catling/Advocate Art; **50–57** Chaaya Prahhat.

Printed in the United Kingdom by Ashford Colour Press Ltd.
Print Number: 04   Print Year: 2022

MIX
Paper from
responsible sources
FSC® C011748